Engaging God's Word
Philippians

Engage Bible Studies
Tools That Transform

Engage Bible Studies
an imprint of

COMMUNITY BIBLE STUDY

Engaging God's Word: Philippians
Copyright © 2012 by Community Bible Study. All rights reserved.
ISBN 978-1-62194-010-4

Published by Community Bible Study
790 Stout Road
Colorado Springs, CO 80921-3802
1-800-826-4181
www.communitybiblestudy.org

Printed in the United States of America.

Contents

Introduction

Welcome to the life-changing adventure of engaging with God's Word!
Whether this is the first time you've opened a Bible or you've studied
the Scriptures all your life, good things are in store for you. Studying
the Bible is unlike any other kind of study you have ever done. That's
because the Word of God is *"living and active"* (Hebrews 4:12) and
transcends time and cultures. The earth and heavens as we know them
will one day pass away, but God's Word never will (Mark 13:31). It's
as relevant to your life today as it was to the people who wrote it down
centuries ago. And the fact that God's Word is living and active means
that reading God's Word is always meant to be a personal experience.
God's Word is not just dead words on a page—it is page after page
of living, powerful words—so get ready, because the time you spend
studying the Bible in this *Engaging God's Word* course will be life-
transforming!

Why Study the Bible?

Some Christians read the Bible because they know they're supposed to.
It's a good thing to do, and God expects it. And all that's true! However,
there are many additional reasons to study God's Word. Here are just
some of them.

We get to know God through His Word. Our God is a relational God
who knows us and wants us to know Him. The Scriptures, which He
authored, reveal much about Him: how He thinks and feels, what His
purposes are, what He thinks about us, how He views the world He
made, what He has planned for the future. The Bible shows us God's
many attributes—His kindness, goodness, justice, love, faithfulness,
mercy, compassion, creativity, redemption, sovereignty, and so on. As
we get to know Him through His Word, we come to love and trust Him.

God speaks to us through His Word. One of the primary ways God speaks to us is through His written Word. Don't be surprised if, as you read the Bible, certain parts nearly jump off the page at you, almost as if they'd been written with you in mind. God is the Author of this incredible book, so that's not just possible, it's likely! Whether it is to find comfort, warning, correction, teaching, or guidance, always approach God's Word with your spiritual ears open (Isaiah 55:3) because God, your loving heavenly Father, has things He wants to say to you.

God's Word brings life. Just about everyone wants to learn the secret to "the good life." And the good news is, that secret is found in God's Word. Don't think of the Bible as a bunch of rules. Viewing it with that mindset is a distortion. God gave us His Word because as our Creator and the Creator of the universe, He alone knows how life was meant to work. He knows that love makes us happier than hate, that generosity brings more joy than greed, and that integrity allows us to rest more peacefully at night than deception does. God's ways are not always "easiest" but they are the way to life. As the Psalmist says, *"If Your law had not been my delight, I would have perished in my affliction. I will never forget Your precepts, for by them You have given me life"* (Psalm 119:92-93).

God's Word offers stability in an unstable world. Truth is an ever-changing negotiable for many people in our culture today. But building your life on constantly changing "truth" is like building your house on shifting sand. God's Word, like God Himself, never changes. What He says was true yesterday, is true today, and will still be true a billion years from now. Jesus said, *"Everyone then who hears these words of Mine and does them will be like a wise man who built his house on the rock"* (Matthew 7:24).

God's Word helps us to pray effectively. When we read God's Word and get to know what He is really like, we understand better how to pray. God answers prayers that are according to His will. We discover His will by reading the Bible. First John 5:14-15 tells us that *"this is the confidence that we have toward Him, that if we ask anything according to His will He hears us. And if we know that He hears us in whatever we ask, we know that we have the requests that we have asked of Him."*

How to Get the Most out of *Engaging God's Word*

Each *Engaging God's Word* study contains key elements that have been carefully designed to help you get the most out of your time in God's Word. Slightly modified for your study-at-home success, this approach is very similar to the tried-and-proven Bible study method that Community Bible Study has used with thousands of men, women, and children across the United States and around the world for nearly 40 years. There are some basic things you can expect to find in each course in this series.

❖ Lesson 1 provides an overview of the Bible book (or books) you will study and questions to help you focus, anticipate, and pray about what you will be learning.

❖ Every lesson contains questions to answer on your own, commentary that reviews and clarifies the passage, and three special sections called "Apply what you have learned," "Think about" and "Personalize this lesson."

❖ Some lessons contain memory verse suggestions.

Whether you plan to use *Engaging God's Word* on your own or with a group, here are some suggestions that will help you enjoy and receive the most benefit from your study.

Spread out each lesson over several days. Your *Engaging God's Word* lessons were designed to take a week to complete. Spreading out your study rather than doing it all at once allows time for the things God is teaching you to sink in and for you to practice applying them.

Pray each time you read God's Word. The Bible is a book unlike any other because God Himself inspired it. The same Spirit who inspired the human authors who wrote it will help you to understand and apply it if you ask Him to. So make it a practice to ask Him to make His Word come alive to you every time you read it.

Read the whole passage covered in the lesson. Before plunging into the questions, take time to read the specific chapter or verses that will be covered in that lesson. Doing this will give you important context for the whole lesson. Reading the Bible in context is an important principle in interpreting it accurately.

Begin learning the memory verse. Learning Scripture by heart requires discipline, but the rewards far outweigh the effort. Memorizing a verse allows you to recall it whenever you need it—for personal encouragement and direction, or to share with someone else. Consider writing the verse on a sticky note or index card that you can post where you will see it often or carry with you to review during the day. Reading and re-reading the verse often—out loud when possible—is a simple way to commit it to memory.

Re-read the passage for each section of questions. Each lesson is divided into sections so that you study one small part of Scripture at a time. Before attempting to answer the questions, review the verses that the questions will cover.

Answer the questions without consulting the Commentary or other reference materials. There is great joy in having the Holy Spirit teach you God's Word on your own, without the help of outside resources. Don't cheat yourself of the delight of discovery by reading the Commentary prematurely. Wait until after you've completed the lesson.

Repeat the process for all the question sections.

Prayerfully consider the "Apply what you have learned," marked with the ⚲ push pin symbol. The vision of Community Bible Study is not to just gain knowledge about the Bible, but to be transformed by it. For this reason, each set of questions closes with a section that encourages you to apply what you are learning. Usually this section involves action—something for you to do. As you practice these suggestions, your life will change.

Read the Commentary. *Engaging God's Word* commentaries are written by theologians whose goal is to help you understand the context of what you are studying as it relates to the rest of Scripture, God's character, and what the passage means for your life. Of necessity, the commentaries include the author's interpretations. While interesting and helpful, keep in mind that the Commentary is simply one person's understanding of what these passages mean. Other godly men and women have views that are also worth considering.

Pause to contemplate each "Think about" section, marked with the ☐ notepad symbol. These features, embedded in the Commentary, offer a place to pause and consider some of the principles being brought out by the text. They provide excellent ideas to journal about or to discuss with other believers, especially those doing the study with you.

Jot down insights or prayer points from the "Personalize this lesson" marked with the ☑ check box symbol. While the "Apply what you have learned" section focuses on doing, the "Personalize this lesson" section focuses on becoming. Spiritual transformation is not just about doing right things and refraining from doing wrong things—it is about changing from the inside out. To be transformed means letting God change our hearts so that our attitudes, emotions, desires, reactions, and goals are increasingly like Jesus'. Often this section will discuss something that you cannot do in your own strength—so your response will usually be something to pray about. Remember that becoming more Christ-like is not just a matter of trying harder—it requires God's empowerment.

Rejoice!
Philippians 1:1-11

Paul's letter to the Philippians is one of his most personal and most passionate. Written to his beloved Philippians from a Roman jail cell, this letter is a kind of "last words." In it, he expresses his deep affection and thankfulness for his children in the faith, summarizes his life's message, and leaves the Philippians with charges and admonitions that will help them continue to grow in Christ. This book, beloved by believers throughout the ages, contains the following themes.

❖ He joyfully thanks the believers for their partnership in spreading the gospel and shares his hopes for their future growth.

❖ He expresses his joy that the gospel is being preached, even through his imprisonment and by those with impure motives.

❖ He urges the Philippians to imitate Christ in living as humble servants.

❖ He gives news of Timothy and Epaphroditus and praises their faithful service.

❖ He proclaims that any gain in this life is worthless compared to knowing and becoming like Christ.

❖ He gives instructions on experiencing peace and contentment in the Lord.

❖ He thanks the Philippians for their financial gifts.

1. Which of the themes you just read about do you most want to learn more about? Why?

   _____

   _____

   _____

   _____

2. Paul clearly demonstrates that joy is possible in any circumstance. What questions do you have about joy and how to experience it?

   _____

   _____

   _____

   _____

3. If you were to write a "last letter," what important lessons from your life in Christ would you want to pass on?

   _____

   _____

   _____

   _____

4. Throughout your study of Philippians, note when *joy* or *rejoicing* are mentioned. Record below the reasons Paul gives for his joy.

   _____

   _____

   _____

   _____

Pause now to take inventory of the joy levels in your life. What gives you joy? Where do you lack it? What makes it hard for you to experience joy? Talk to God about what you discover. If you are doing this study with a small group, share your thoughts with your group, and pray for one another.

Rejoice!
Philippians 1:1-11

Philippians is often called the "Joy Book." Although Paul is writing from prison, he uses the words *joy* or *rejoice* at least 14 times. His joy depends on Jesus, not on his surroundings. In this letter, Paul thanks the Philippian church for their ongoing financial support and reports on his circumstances. He elevates Christ in His beauty and power, and encourages believers to live victoriously.

The Author

God chose Paul, a Jew trained as a rabbi, to take the good news about Jesus to the Gentiles. Meeting the risen Christ had changed his life forever. At great physical, financial, and emotional cost, Paul traveled the world preaching the gospel. He uses the word *gospel* seven times in this letter. He also writes repeatedly of fellowship. To him, *fellowship* means partnership, not a social experience.

The Date

Paul probably wrote his letters between AD 50 and AD 62. The best evidence suggests he wrote this letter to the Philippians while under house arrest in Rome—so scholars place the date of Philippians around AD 60. As he awaited Caesar's decision on his fate, Paul did not know what his future would hold. He faced life or death victoriously "in Christ."

Paul's History With the Philippians

On Paul's second missionary journey, Paul and Silas traveled to Syria and Cilicia, Derbe, and Lystra. Timothy joined them at Lystra (Acts 16:1-3). Following two unsuccessful attempts to go into Asia Minor, Paul had a vision: A Macedonian man begged him, *"Come over to Macedonia and help us"* (16:9). Paul and his companions sailed to Philippi, a leading city of the district of Macedonia (present-day Greece) and a Roman colony (16:12).

On the Sabbath, Paul and his party went out to the riverside. Some women were there, including Lydia, a successful businesswoman from Thyatira. She and her household became Paul's first converts in Philippi. Contrary to the cultural norms of that time, women were prominent in the early church. In the closing remarks of Paul's letter to the Romans, Paul mentions several women who played an important role in the church (Romans 16:1-16). Paul eagerly accepted them as fellow workers in the kingdom and elevated and dignified their position.

When Paul drove out a demon from a Greek slave girl, ending her lucrative fortune telling, her angry owners started a riot (Acts 16:19). Paul and Silas were jailed. At midnight, their feet in stocks, they were singing hymns when an earthquake shook the prison and freed them. The jailer was about to take his own life, because the Romans would have killed him if any prisoner escaped, but Paul reassured him that the prisoners were still there. Before morning, the jailer's entire family was baptized as Christians. Learning that Paul was a Roman citizen, the magistrates came to the prison, apologized, and asked Paul and Silas to leave the city. After a visit to Lydia's house to encourage the new Christians, they went on their way.

The ties between Paul and the church at Philippi remained close. During his long stay at Ephesus, he sent Timothy to the Macedonian churches. Acts 20:1-2 reports that Paul visited these churches, including the one in Philippi, on his way to Corinth. He later visited Philippi again and spent the Passover season there before his last journey to Jerusalem.

The Philippians were special to Paul because they were kind to him and his associates from the beginning. Paul's first convert, Lydia, welcomed his team into her home. The Philippians sent Paul support when he was in Thessalonica and during his imprisonment in Rome. They likely joined other Macedonian churches in contributing to the relief fund for the Jerusalem Christians.

Friendly Greetings

Paul begins this letter with the title *servant,* acknowledging that he belongs to Jesus as a slave bought with His blood. Paul calls recipients of this letter *"all the saints in Christ Jesus who are at Philippi"* (Philippians

1:1). The Greek word for *saints* is from the word *holy*. It means set apart for a specific purpose—in this case, for God's specific purpose.

Paul's greeting to the Philippian Christians is one he often used: *"Grace to you and peace from God our Father and the Lord Jesus Christ"* (1:2). The Greek word for *grace* means *joy, beauty, and pleasure*. God's grace makes it possible for every Christian to exhibit these traits. The word for *peace* implies the total well-being of a person, community, or nation. The biblical idea of peace is more than the absence of war. It suggests harmony, stability, and serenity. God desires Christians to live in harmony with Him, with others, and within themselves.

> **Think about** the word Paul used for *grace* in verse 2 (see paragraph above), and substitute "joy, beauty, and pleasure" for *grace* as you read the verse. What perspective does this provide on what God desires for your life?

A Joyful Prayer

Paul's prayers for the Philippians are joyful, he says, because of their active partnership with him from the moment they believed. He bases his joy on their history and on his confidence that God will continue to work in and through them. Paul can write joyful prayers because he has learned to trust God. He is confident because he has experienced God's faithfulness.

In 1:9-11, Paul tells his readers he wants their love to keep growing, along with *"knowledge and all discernment,"* so they might identify the highest and best for their lives. This prayer shows profound insight into what they—and all believers—need. Love without knowledge and insight can be sentimentality, while knowledge and insight without love can be arrogant and harsh.

Personalize this lesson.

Even in prison, Paul was full of the joy found in Christ alone. It's often tempting to think we would be happier if our circumstances were different. But Paul shows us that real joy is a matter of delighting in Christ and is not dependent on outward conditions.

Are there any "prisons" in your life—any circumstances in which you feel trapped, or would like to change? What can you learn from Paul about how to experience joy in less than ideal conditions?

Paul's Personal Testimony
Philippians 1:12-30

Memorize God's Word: Philippians 1:21.

❖ Review Philippians 1:1-11—Greeting and Prayer

1. In 1:1, Paul refers to Timothy and himself as *"servants"* and to the Philippian believers as *"saints."* How did Paul see himself in relationship to the Philippian believers?

   _____

   _____

   _____

   _____

2. From Paul's prayer (1:9-11), what results does he want to see in believers' lives?

   _____

   _____

   _____

   _____

3. According to this prayer, what is the ultimate goal for all believers?

   _____

   _____

   _____

   _____

❖ Philippians 1:12-14—Paul's Way of Evangelism

4. How has Paul's imprisonment influenced the palace guard? (See also 4:22.)

    _____

    _____

5. Explain how and why Paul's imprisonment strengthened the believers.

    _____

    _____

6. What can you learn from this passage about

    a. Paul's priorities? _____

    _____

    b. His attitude toward his imprisonment? _____

    _____

    _____

    c. His confidence in God?_____

    _____

    _____

❖ Philippians 1:15-18—Motives for Preaching

7. What motivations for preaching Christ does Paul mention?

    _____

    _____

    _____

8. How would you describe Paul's attitude toward those preaching the gospel from wrong motives?

    _____

    _____

    _____

❖ Philippians 1:19-26—Paul's Expectations

9. a. Through what two means does Paul say he will be delivered from his situation?

    _____

    _____

    _____

    b. Describe a time when you have experienced deliverance through the power of one of these forces.

    _____

    _____

    _____

    _____

10. a. Paul feels torn by two options: life or death. From his perspective, what is desirable about each?

    _____

    _____

    _____

    b. How does he resolve this apparent conflict?

    _____

    _____

❖ Philippians 1:27-30—Paul's Exhortation

11. a. Who are some of the opponents of the gospel today?

    _____

    _____

    b. How might you suffer for telling others about Jesus?

    _____

    _____

    _____

12. Paul implies in 1:27-28 that Satan conquers believers by dividing them and diverting their focus from spreading the gospel. What does standing firm, being united with other believers, and being fearless say to our enemies?

_____

_____

13. a. According to 1:27-30, what are the characteristics of a godly lifestyle? (See also Ephesians 4:1-3.)

_____

_____

_____

b. Which of the above characteristics best describes you? In which do you most need to grow? Talk with God about it.

_____

_____

_____

_____

Apply what you have learned. God's Word tells us to experience and demonstrate a joyful attitude in the midst of positive *and* negative circumstances. Think of an area of your life that is difficult right now. List some practical ways you can conduct yourself in a manner *"worthy of the gospel of Christ"* (Philippians 1:27) in that situation.

Paul's Personal Testimony
Philippians 1:12-30

A Prisoner and Yet …

In Acts, Luke describes Paul's house arrest in Rome. Though he was chained to a guard, Paul could still have visitors and share about Jesus (28:16, 30). God Himself planned the most effective strategy for His servant Paul—including his imprisonment, which actually helped *"to advance the gospel"* (Philippians 1:12). The Praetorian guards, who had great influence among people of all social strata, heard Paul's preaching daily for two years (Acts 28:30-31). Many of them became Christians (Philippians 4:22). God's unusual strategy also strengthened Paul's fellow believers. They increased in courage and preached the gospel wherever they were.

Think about the freedom believers have in Christ. Bondage to sin is the real imprisonment; Christ frees us from that bondage. Paul's faith and peace grew out of his knowledge that he was free in the only way that really counts—in the spiritual sense.

Spiritual Discernment

Paul says he knows that some are preaching more to annoy him than to honor Christ, but to him the important thing is that Christ is being preached. How can he be so calm about this? In other situations, he lashed out at those who were teaching inappropriately. For example, in Galatia, some Jews began teaching that, in order to be "real" Christians, Gentile believers must be circumcised and keep certain parts of the Jewish Law (Acts 15). This teaching was not only contrary to Jesus' own preaching but to the whole meaning of the gospel. The church's future depended on expelling the false belief that Christ's death on the cross was insufficient payment for sin.

Although their motives may be wrong, the rivals Paul mentions in 1:15-18 are preaching the same gospel as Paul. He remains calm because his concern is not with purity of motive but with purity of message.

Joyful Living

Paul's life purpose is to show Christ to the world. Because this is his reason for living, he can say: *"For to me to live is Christ, and to die is gain"* (Philippians 1:21). To die means being with the Lord he lives to serve. While he still has time on earth, Paul is determined to glorify Christ.

Paul models his own advice to Timothy: *"Preach the word; be ready in season and out of season; reprove, rebuke, and exhort, with complete patience and teaching"* (2 Timothy 4:2). As long as he lives, he intends to speak the truth, honoring Christ with his words and his life, confident that he will have the courage to live or die in a way that honors Him. Yet he is torn by his conflicting desires to die and be with Christ or live for the sake of others. The word he uses for *torn* describes a ship going through a narrow canal. Paul feels hemmed in between two glorious options: To *"depart and be with Christ"* (Philippians 1:23) would be to enjoy total freedom, relieved of the burden of life on earth. The Greek word for *"depart"* means *to loose,* as in untying ropes or pulling up a ship's anchor. Death would release him to move on, to set sail toward a glorious, eternal destination. Instead, Paul is convinced he will *"remain"* (1:25).

Think about Paul's conflicting desires. He longed to go to be with Christ, yet he hated to think of leaving young believers. He loved life, yet he looked forward to death. These are only two of the paradoxes of the Christian life. We, like Paul, can experience joy in the midst of heartbreak. We experience sorrow and suffering, but are glad in Christ. Although the storms of life threaten to overwhelm us, we can stay calm. And, like Paul, we can love to live, yet long to die. In the best of all paradoxes, knowing Christ makes us love life more and fear death less.

Citizens of Christ's Kingdom

"Only let your manner of life be worthy of the gospel of Christ" (Philippians 1:27). Held in Rome, chained to a Praetorian guard, Paul tried to convince his guards as well as the Philippians of God's truth. The Philippian church must have had vivid memories of Paul's first stay, when he and Silas were beaten and jailed without a trial. When the authorities wanted to release them quietly, Paul announced that he was a Roman citizen who had been unjustly jailed; he demanded proper treatment. Being a Roman citizen carried many privileges. The alarmed magistrates personally apologized to them and asked them to leave the city (Acts 16:37-39).

Just as Roman citizens had privileges and obligations, so do citizens of heaven. The Philippians' ability to stand firm, their unity, and their lack of fear would be a sign to those who opposed them. When we live like believers, it validates our message. Finally, when Paul says suffering for the sake of Christ is a privilege, he is restating what Jesus said in Matthew 5:10-12: We are blessed when we suffer for the gospel's sake.

Personalize this lesson.

Are our lives *"worthy of the gospel of Christ"* (Philippians 1:27)? As believers, we are to love, honor, and obey Him. If we truly follow Christ, we will honor Him in our thoughts, words, and actions. People will see His indwelling presence in our lives as we live and move in Him. Jesus said others will know we are His followers because of our love for one another (John 13:35). We have peace with God and with one another through Christ's love and forgiveness (Ephesians 2:13-18). Therefore we are to reflect His peace in our relationships. Our unity in Christ is a living testimony.

Think about your relationships with other believers. Is there someone in your small group, serving with you in ministry, or just with whom you have regular contact, who rubs you the wrong way? Ask God to show you how you could honor Christ in your thoughts, words, and actions as you interact with that person.

Christ: The Supreme Model
Philippians 2:1-11

Memorize God's Word: Philippians 2:9-11.

❖ Philippians 2:1-11—A Worthy Role Model

1. What does it mean for someone to be our Ultimate Model?

   _____

   _____

2. What words and phrases in 2:6-8 describe what Christ did as our Ultimate Model?

   _____

   _____

   _____

3. Keeping in mind what Paul has said in the letter up to this point, why do you think he places such emphasis on Christ as our model?

   _____

   _____

❖ Philippians 2:1-2—Plea for Unity

4. What has Paul already said in chapter 1 that would help the Philippians understand his references in 2:1 concerning

   a. *"in Christ"* (see 1:6)?_____

   _____

    b.   *"comfort from love"* (see 1:9)? _____

            _____

    c.   *"affection and sympathy"* (see 1:7)? _____

            _____

5. a.   In Philippians 2:2, what does Paul ask the Philippians to do?

            _____

            _____

    b.   Why do you think Paul stresses *"being of the same mind"* (2:2)? (See also 1:27; 4:2.)

            _____

            _____

            _____

❖ Philippians 2:2-5—The Way to Achieve Unity

6.   How do the ideals in 2:2 and the attitudes and actions in 2:3-4 relate to each other?

            _____

            _____

            _____

            _____

7.   Summarize what Paul writes in the following passages, and tell how each parallels Philippians 2:3-5:

    a.   Ephesians 4:3-6, 31-32 _____

            _____

            _____

    b.   Colossians 3:12-15 _____

            _____

            _____

❖ Philippians 2:6-8—The Attitude of Christ

8.　a.　Christ is identified as *"being in very nature God"* (2:6, NIV). How do John 1:1 and Colossians 1:15-20 support this statement?

_____

_____

_____

　　b.　How is Christ like us? (See also Hebrews 4:15.)

_____

_____

_____

9.　As you grow in Christ, you will imitate His attitude of humility and servanthood more and more. How might that change a relationship or circumstance that is currently troublesome or challenging?

_____

_____

_____

10.　What do you think it took for Jesus to empty Himself and make Himself nothing (2:7)?

_____

_____

_____

_____

❖ Philippians 2:9-11—Christ's Exaltation

11.　What does the word *"therefore"* in 2:9 tell you about why Christ is exalted?

_____

_____

12. What can we expect when we humble ourselves? (See also 1 Peter 5:6.)

_____

_____

_____

13. What is Jesus' role now (Hebrews 7:25)?

_____

_____

_____

14. In the future, who will bow at His name and confess that He is Lord (2:10-11)?

_____

_____

_____

 Apply what you have learned. Thoughtfully consider what Christ's options were and what He chose—for your sake. Write Him a thank-you note.

Christ: The Supreme Model
Philippians 2:1-11

Paul is deeply concerned about the lack of love and unity in the Philippian church. A church in conflict is not God's plan for His body and destroys its witness. Conflicts also deprive believers of fellowship and support.

Directive and Directions

Aware of their problems, Paul gives the Philippians a directive in 2:2 and directions for achieving it in 2:3-4. Instead of telling them to try harder to be more loving, he points to Christ as the perfect example of living in a way that promotes loving relationships.

Early Christian communities consisted of people from many cultures and backgrounds. Paul wants them to achieve unity in diversity. Note the words he uses in appealing to their resources in Christ (2:1):

- ❖ *"encouragement,"* meaning consolation, exhortation
- ❖ *"comfort,"* gentleness, cheer
- ❖ *"participation in the Spirit,"* support, partnership
- ❖ *"affection,"* tender affection
- ❖ *"sympathy,"* kindness in relieving sorrow and want

Paul knows that Christian maturity involves living in harmony with people unlike ourselves. In urging his readers to agree, he uses two Greek words meaning *harmony of soul* and *being of one opinion*. Achieving such harmony requires unity around a common goal—and it does not happen overnight. In many ways, it is like blending musical instruments for harmony. In the same way, the Christian community's purpose is to glorify God. When personalities and backgrounds harmonize into a lovely symphony under God's direction, the differences produce the beauty.

Problems in the Church

The specific problems Paul addresses are timeless: selfish ambition, conceit, looking to our own interests, lack of humility. Paul tells the Philippians to *"in humility count others more significant than yourselves"* (2:3) and focus on *"the interests of others"* (2:4).

Think about how selfishness and egotism do not automatically disappear when we become Christians. We must deal with egotism daily. In Philippians 2:3-4, Paul tells us to put others first and to control our actions and attitudes. Christ's command to love one another (John 15:12) tells us to take action, not to feel a warm emotion. We can decide every day to obey Christ by putting others' well-being above our own. We can replace pride with humility as we depend on Him to enable us to be like Him.

Paul begins an important theological passage in 2:5. He has been encouraging the Philippians to rid the church of problems caused by selfishness. He urges them to look out for each other and illustrates his point by telling them to consider Jesus as their example. Philippians 2:6-11 is often called "The Hymn to Christ"; many scholars think the early church sang these verses. Paul describes Jesus as *"being in very nature God"* (2:6, NIV), using a Greek word for *"being"* that means *to begin, belong, exist.* In other words, Jesus was God from the beginning.

Paul chooses the Greek word for *nature* that means *the essential, unchangeable being of God in Christ.* Christ was and is truly God. John's Gospel states, *"In the beginning was the Word, and the Word was with God, and the Word was God"* (John 1:1). John used a term familiar to Jews and Greeks, *"the Word"* (Greek *Logos*), to clarify Christ's identity. To the Jews, *the Word* was associated with their all-powerful, wise God. To the Greeks, *the Word* was the rational power that gave order to the universe. John is saying that Jesus Christ encompasses both qualities and much more. Truth comes from God in the person of His Son, Jesus Christ. Jesus is the true *Logos.* Although fully God, Christ exercised humility and did not cling to His rights as God when He walked the earth. He could have paraded His glory before His opponents, but He never did. Nor did He try to grab the glory that would be His after the Cross. Instead, He humbled Himself to obey His Father completely, choosing to die a humiliating, agonizing death because His will and the Father's will were one. He *"emptied Himself"* (Philippians 2:7), from a word meaning *to empty like a bottle, to strip oneself of all privileges.* He describes His mission this way: *"The Son of Man came not to be served but to serve, and to give His life as a ransom for 'many'"* (Mark 10:45).

Jesus was made in human likeness. He was a real man, no mere phantom as some declared. He gave up all the advantages of His position in the Godhead. It is as if a king's son came to town as a common citizen, leaving behind his crown and his servants. Yet the blood of a king would still flow in his veins. Jesus had to be both God and man to reconcile man with God.

Think about how God's way of doing things upsets all our ideas about power. Jesus came to earth in humility and took the role of the lowest of servants. When He used His power it was not for Himself but for the sake of others and to bring glory to His Father. His miracles were not meant to impress but to prove His claim to be God.

The Glorious Name

God leads His followers to glory through the path of humility. The word *"therefore"* in 2:9 connects exaltation with humility and humiliation. Because Jesus humbly obeyed the Father, God gave Him the name *"that is above every name"* (2:9). In biblical times, names were given seriously and prayerfully, but were sometimes changed according to the situation or need—often reflecting a significant spiritual experience. For example, God changed Abram's name (*exalted father*) to Abraham (*ancestor of many nations*) when He established His covenant with him (Genesis 17:1-8). In the closing stanzas of the Philippians passage, God honors Jesus and gives Him the name *"Lord"* (Philippians 2:11). Paul uses the same Greek word for *Lord* as the Old Testament translations used for *Yahweh*, again asserting Jesus' deity. One day, as predicted in Isaiah 45:23, every knee will bow and every tongue confess that Jesus is Lord.

Personalize this lesson.

✓ Jesus is our model of obedience and humility in words and actions. He is also our model of exaltation—God raised Him to the place of highest honor. There is a relationship between humility and exaltation: God lifts up those who are humble. He promises that we will appear with Jesus in glory (Colossians 3:4) and one day be like Him (1 John 3:2). That is our future. Our task now is to live humbly before God and others the same way Jesus did. He did not exalt Himself; He exalted God. And in turn, God exalted Him. God promises to do the same for us (1 Samuel 2:30).

How can we grow in humility? One way to identify pride in ourselves is to examine areas in which we have trouble obeying. Think of a few biblical commands with which you repeatedly struggle. How does pride enter in here? For example, when we complain, the root cause might be thinking that we know better than God how our lives should be. Ask God to show you any areas of pride you need to deal with, and ask Him to help you humble yourself when temptations arise.

Workers in the Kingdom
Philippians 2:12-30

❖ Philippians 2:12-13—God's Part and Our Part

1. According to your understanding, what is salvation, and how can a person receive it (John 3:16; Romans 10:9-10)?

   _____

   _____

   _____

   _____

   _____

   _____

2. Read James 2:14-26 to see what Paul means by *"work out your own salvation"* (2:12). What is the relationship between faith and works?

   _____

   _____

   _____

3. a. According to this passage, what is the source of motivation and power as you *"work out your own salvation"*?

   _____

   _____

   _____

   _____

b. How does the fact that the God is working within you to help you grow encourage you?

_____

_____

_____

❖ Philippians 2:14-18—The Right Attitude

4. According to Romans 12:1-2, what is the key to living out Philippians 2:14-18?

_____

_____

5. As God empowers you to obey Him (2:13), what attitudes will characterize your life (2:14-16)?

_____

_____

_____

_____

6. As you grow in these areas, how might your family and professional relationships be affected? Be specific.

_____

_____

_____

_____

7. What is the secret of Paul's ability to rejoice in light of the danger and uncertainty of his situation?

_____

_____

_____

_____

❖ Philippians 2:19-24—Paul and Timothy

8. What does this passage tell you about

    a. Paul's relationship (personal and professional) with Timothy? (See also 1 Timothy 1:2.) _____

    _____

    _____

    b. Paul's relationship with the Philippians? _____

    _____

    _____

9. What clues can you find in this Scripture about the manner in which Timothy

    a. honors God? _____

    _____

    _____

    _____

    b. serves others? _____

    _____

    _____

    _____

❖ Philippians 2:25-30—Paul and Epaphroditus

10. What roles does Epaphroditus fill as he relates to Paul (2:25)?

    _____

    _____

11. How would you describe the relationship between Epaphroditus and the Philippians?

    _____

    _____

    _____

12. Paul beautifully demonstrates Philippians 2:1-4 by praising Timothy and Epaphroditus. Is there someone's godly character or behavior you could tell others about?

_____

_____

_____

13. Read 1 Corinthians 3:5-8. Paul identifies his fellow workers as *"servants"* (1 Corinthians 3:5). How does this term unite believers who work together for God?

_____

_____

_____

14. As we imitate Jesus, what does it mean for us to take *"the form of a servant"* (Philippians 2:6-7)?

_____

_____

_____

Apply what you have learned. The entire second chapter of Philippians deals with selfless servanthood, an idea that challenges today's concepts of identity, purpose, and personal rights.

Think about what is on your schedule for tomorrow (or another day this week). For every segment of your day, imagine what it would be like if you took on the attitude and actions of a servant. How would you treat people? How hard would you work? What might you do differently? How might your attitude change? Write down some ideas.

With God's help, carry out as many of those ideas as possible as you go through your day.

Workers in the Kingdom
Philippians 2:12-30

Cooperation

Paul has been urging unity and the behavior that produces it. His hymn of praise to Christ as our perfect example leads him to instruct the Philippians in how to apply Christ's humble obedience in their lives. He begins Philippians 2:12 with the connecting link *"therefore."* Paul is saying, "You should be like Him; do as He did." In spite of the fact that Paul cannot come to visit them, he urges the Philippians to continue to *"work out* [their] *own salvation with fear and trembling"* (2:12). This verse, often taken out of context, has caused confusion in the church. It sounds as if Paul is asking people to produce their own salvation by working— which is impossible.

Nowhere in the Bible is the paradox of divine sovereignty and human free will more obvious than in verses 12 and 13. Neither truth can be denied: God *is* in control. People *do* have real choices with consequences. The maturing and perfecting of a Christian is a cooperative effort. The phrase *"work out"* is from the Greek word *katergazomai*, meaning *to bring out as a result, to practice, to complete what has been started*. In this context, Paul is speaking about something God starts in the believer's life that the believer responds to. Like the earth, which God created and man is to cultivate, Christians are to participate in bringing their salvation to completion. *"For it is God who works* [Greek *energein*] *in you"* (Philippians 2:13), Paul continues. He uses the word *energein*, meaning *active energy, effective power*, to describe how God moves believers to want to choose God's way and then enables them to do so.

> **Think about** how God has already saved us from
> the *penalty* of sin; He is saving us now from the *power*
> of sin; and He will save us from the *presence* of sin.
> Verse 12 does *not* endorse the idea that salvation can
> be earned. Even Paul admitted he could not do what he
> knew—and wanted—to do (Romans 7:15-23). But God,
> through Jesus, enables us to live victoriously (7:24-25). The
> initiative always belongs to God. God gives, we receive. God
> creates, we cultivate. God saves, we respond.

A Christian Lifestyle

Paul stresses the importance of Christlike attitudes: *"Do all things without grumbling or disputing"* (Philippians 2:14). Christians who don't humbly and willingly obey God often grumble about their circumstances. Paul says they should not respond that way or argue with each other so that they might become pure. He establishes a cause-and-effect relationship between attitudes and behavior. Wrong attitudes pollute behavior so that it is impossible to become pure. God wants His children to live *"blameless"* (2:15) lives despite the wickedness of their generation and their world. Then they will *"shine as lights in the world, holding fast to the word of life"* (2:15-16) like a torch to light the way for others to follow.

Paul longs to feel proud of the Philippians. He has worked hard on their behalf, is now in prison because of his missionary activity, and does not want to feel he has labored in vain. Their good lives cause Paul to rejoice—even if he were to die as a martyr.

Paul's Fellow Workers

Paul's young associate Timothy—the child of a marriage between a Greek (Gentile) man and a devout Jewish believer, Eunice (Acts 16:1; 2 Timothy 1:5)—was nurtured in the faith by his mother and his grandmother, Lois. Paul and Silas first associated with Timothy when they came to his hometown on their second missionary journey. Paul calls Timothy his spiritual son (1 Timothy 1:2).

When the missionaries left Lystra, Timothy accompanied them through Phrygia, Galatia, and Europe. He was dedicated to the cause of Christ and ministered on Paul's behalf to the churches in Macedonia, Corinth, Philippi, Thessalonica, and Ephesus. He joined Paul in writing letters to the Christians in Philippi, Colossae, and Thessalonica and served as Paul's secretary in writing the first letter to the Corinthians. In spite of his youth (1 Timothy 4:12) and frequent illnesses (5:23), Timothy served God well and worked faithfully with Paul, who believed no one was as dependable and genuinely concerned about the Philippians' welfare as Timothy.

Think about how Paul does not record information about Timothy's appearance or abilities. God looks at a person's inner character rather than the outward image (1 Samuel 16:7). To God, and to Paul, Timothy's important qualities were his commitment to Jesus, his willingness to walk into danger for the sake of the gospel, and his service to fellow believers. He had learned to look beneath the surface and get to know the real person, the one in whom Christ is living and working.

Paul describes Epaphroditus as an *apostolos*, a word sometimes used in the New Testament for messengers sent by the churches, responsible for handling contributions and finances. The congregation in Philippi had sent Epaphroditus with their contribution for Paul. Little is known of his background, but Paul's words reveal his integrity and dedication. Epaphroditus had been so critically ill while in Rome with Paul that he was *"near to death"* (Philippians 2:27), but he still wanted to stay and support Paul in any way possible. Paul calls him *"my brother and fellow worker and fellow soldier"* (2:25), describing their relationship and Epaphroditus's willingness to share the danger from enemies of the gospel. Epaphroditus ministers to Paul, who appeals to the Philippians: *"Receive him in the Lord with all joy, and honor such men, for he nearly died for the work of Christ, risking his life to complete what was lacking in your service to me"* (2:29-30). Though mentioned only in this brief passage, Epaphroditus is worthy of honor.

Personalize this lesson.

Christians are to live and *"work out"* the salvation God has given us in Christ. But Paul discovered that few people are willing to be servants—of God or of other people. In writing about Timothy, Paul comments, *"I have no one like him, who will be genuinely concerned for your welfare. For they all seek their own interests, not those of Jesus Christ"* (Philippians 2:20-21).

Jesus said that He came *"not to be served but to serve"* (Matthew 20:28), and taught His disciples to have the same attitude. When do you find it easiest to serve others? In what circumstances do you find it most difficult?

Ask God to show you any barriers in your heart to serving. Then ask Him to help you humble yourself, surrender your own interests, and pursue Jesus' priorities with greater passion.

Moving Toward the Goal
Philippians 3

Memorize God's Word: Philippians 3:8.

❖ Philippians 3:1-3—Paul's Warning

1. Based on the study so far, write a biblical definition of *joy.*

   _____

   _____

2. Explain the spiritual significance of circumcision (Genesis 17:9-11; Deuteronomy 10:16; 30:6).

   _____

   _____

3. a. According to Romans 2:28-29, what is "true" circumcision?

   _____

   _____

   b. What three identifying traits of truly circumcised people does Paul suggest to the Philippians (3:3)?

   _____

   _____

4. Note the terms Paul applies to those who depend on physical circumcision (3:2). Why do you think Paul uses such harsh words?

   _____

   _____

❖ Philippians 3:4-7—Paul's Testimony

5. What reasons does Paul have for putting *"confidence in the flesh"* (3:4-6)?

    _____

    _____

6. In the context in which Paul uses the word, what do you think he means by *"flesh"*?

    _____

    _____

7. How does Paul view his *"credentials,"* and why (3:7-8)? (See also 2 Corinthians 5:17.)

    _____

    _____

8. How can we know if we are trusting in our own abilities and accomplishments instead of in God? How can we keep these things in proper perspective?

    _____

    _____

❖ Philippians 3:8-11—Paul's Priorities

9. Paul considers *"everything as loss"* (3:8) compared to knowing Jesus. How is the value you place on knowing Jesus reflected in your priorities and schedule? Do you need to make any adjustments? If so, what?

    _____

    _____

10. The Greek word for *know* indicates experiencing, not just knowledge. With this in mind, reread 3:8-11. What does Paul want to experience (*"know"*) in his relationship with Christ?

    _____

    _____

❖ Philippians 3:12-16—Paul's Progress

11. a. What stands out to you as Paul reveals that he has not *"obtained this"* (3:12)?

_____

_____

b. Why does he *"press on"*?

_____

_____

c. How can this encourage us? (See also Philippians 1:6.)

_____

_____

12. a. From Hebrews 12:1-2, a parallel passage, explain what is involved in effectively *"running the race."*

_____

_____

b. Why is the principle of forgetting past sins (3:13) so important? (See also 1 John 1:9.)

_____

_____

13. Philippians 3:12-16 states Paul's life purpose. Write a statement expressing your life purpose.

_____

_____

❖ Philippians 3:17-21—Paul's Pattern

14. Paul is so confident of God's work in his life that he encourages others to imitate him. Describe how the Philippians could do this.

_____

_____

15. How does Paul describe *"enemies of the cross of Christ"* (3:18)?

_____

_____

16. a.   Of what great facts does Paul remind us in 3:20-21? (See also 1 John 3:2.)

_____

_____

b.   What is one way you can remind yourself that you are a citizen of heaven and live accordingly?

_____

_____

Apply what you have learned. Jesus Christ is *"the resurrection and the life,"* and we who believe in Him will never die (John 11:25). Our resurrected, living Lord is coming back to restore us in beauty and perfection—to make us like Him! But we don't have to wait: 2 Corinthians 3:18 says we *"are being"* transformed into his image bit by bit already, as we *"behold the glory of the Lord."*

What are some ways in which you can *"behold the glory of the Lord"* in your daily life? Through Bible study and meditation? Worship? Prayer? Serving others? Choose one new method of beholding Jesus, or one you haven't practiced lately, and incorporate it into your schedule this week.

Moving Toward the Goal
Philippians 3

The Repeated Refrain

"Finally, my brothers, rejoice in the Lord," Paul writes (Philippians 3:1). The Lord is the only real source of joy and comfort. Relying too much on God's good gifts—health, security, the love of family and friends—rather than on God Himself invites disaster, because the gifts last only for a time. When believers rejoice in the Lord, they can thank Him for all His goodness with or without His gifts. Paul believes it is necessary to continually remind the Philippians of the importance of that attitude.

Warning of False Teaching

Next, Paul warns them: *"Look out for the dogs ... who mutilate the flesh"* (3:2). He is referring to those who teach that to be Christians, Gentiles must first be circumcised. Originally, God introduced circumcision as a covenant sign (Genesis 17:9-11), not merely a religious ritual. Later, God made it clear that circumcision represents the change of heart that comes when people genuinely turn to Him. Scripture often reminds God's people of the necessity of a "circumcised heart" (Deuteronomy 30:6; Romans 2:28-29). Only true circumcision—a change of the heart—leads to genuine worship of God.

Paul's Testimony

Paul's family, cultural, religious, and educational background (Philippians 3:5-6) is impressive:

- ❖ *"circumcised on the eighth day"*—Circumcision is a covenant sign of true Judaism.
- ❖ *"of the people of Israel"*—Paul is a direct descendant of Abraham, Isaac, and Jacob, a bloodline blessed by God.

- ❖ *"of the tribe of Benjamin"*—This tribe produced the first king, Saul (1 Samuel 9:1-2).
- ❖ *"a Hebrew of Hebrews"*—Paul spoke fluent Hebrew.
- ❖ *"a Pharisee"*—Paul had segregated himself from the common people.
- ❖ *"as to zeal, a persecutor of the church"*—As a sign of sincere religious fervor, Paul persecuted Christians but later regretted his actions (1 Corinthians 15:9).
- ❖ *"as to righteousness under the law, blameless"*—The Greek word for faultless means without blemish, perfect, excellent.

But Paul puts *"no confidence in the flesh"* (Philippians 3:3). *"Flesh"* refers to the whole person apart from Christ, not the physical body. Paul considers all his credentials worthless compared to knowing Christ. He speaks strongly against relying on talents and advantages because he knows they could become false gods and perhaps already had—luring the Philippians away from trust in Jesus alone. It is impossible to trust in our own resources and at the same time rely totally on Christ. Paul recognizes that his credentials— compared to Christ's righteousness and sacrificial death—are nothing.

Think about the temptation to rely on ourselves—our background, intellect, beauty, or possessions. Remember what Paul wrote: Our assets have nothing to do with spirituality. They are good gifts from God, but trusting in them is worthless. Anything in which we place our confidence, other than Christ, must be rejected and discarded—thrown away like trash.

Paul states his life goal—*"to know* [Greek *ginosko*] *Christ." Ginosko* means *the experiential knowledge a lover has of the loved one,* not just mental knowledge. Paul possesses mental knowledge of what God has declared to be true about believers, and he preaches these truths (Romans 6:2-14; Colossians 2:12-13; 3:1). But his deeper longing is to *experience* these truths. He wants the same power that brought Jesus out of the grave.

Paul strives toward his goal, recommending it to the Philippian believers. The fact that not even Paul has "arrived" spiritually is not discouraging because the entire New Testament teaches that we do not reach perfection until we enter heaven. Paul, like all Christians, was in process.

Next, Paul warns against those who promise perfection by observing Jewish Law or gaining some "secret knowledge." Some people believed these false teachings and tried to add them to the Christian faith. Paul makes it clear that perfection cannot be attained through those methods.

Think about how Paul's words—*"straining," "press on"*—(3:13-14) imply tremendous effort. How did he do that without becoming proud? The key is in 3:13: *"One thing I do: forgetting what lies behind."* He meant forgetting not only the failures and sins, but the successes. When we look back on a difficult time we have come through by trusting Jesus, a trial suffered for His sake without faltering or complaining, or being used as a witness in someone's life, we may be tempted to congratulate ourselves. Instead, we must thank God for His grace, not rely on past success, and keep moving forward toward the goal Christ has set for us.

Not only does Paul refuse to look back, he strains to move forward, to fulfill God's plan for his life and accomplish the things Christ had in mind when He took hold of him on the Damascus Road (Acts 9:3-6). After making clear his goal and the fact that he is not yet perfect, Paul advises the Philippians to *"join in imitating me"* (Philippians 3:17). He means imitate his commitment to Christ, not every detail of his life. He refers again to the *"enemies of the cross of Christ"* (3:18) with tenderness and tears, but also with harshness. These men are trying to earn acceptance with God, which Paul sees as a dangerous temptation—more deadly than overt sin.

Paul is necessarily severe toward all who offer ways of gaining God's acceptance other than trusting in Christ—they preach a false gospel. These *"dogs"* (Philippians 3:2) and *"enemies of the cross"* (3:18) are not the same men mentioned in 1:15, who preached a true gospel. Paul did not worry about them. But when the truth of the gospel is undermined, he is unbending. Paul ends chapter 3 by giving clear reasons to avoid all the traps that cause believers to turn from dependence on Jesus. He reminds them that their residence here is temporary and their final destination certain. He promises that Christ has the power to bring all believers to perfection.

Personalize this lesson.

Paul modeled his thoughts, words, and actions on Christ. He invited believers to *"join in imitating me, and keep your eyes on those who walk according to the example you have in us"* (3:17). If we follow Christ closely and obey Him willingly, we, too, will be good role models for others. Remember, though, that moving toward this goal is a process (Romans 12:2).

How are you doing as a role model? What areas of your life would other believers do well to imitate? If you have difficulty answering this question, ask a friend or family member for ideas.

What areas are not yet ready for others to imitate? Ask God to show you one area that He would like to begin to transform. Talk with Him about how you can work together to become more like Jesus in this area.

Unity and Charity
Philippians 4

Memorize God's Word: Philippians 4:6.

❖ Philippians 4:1-3—Plea for Peace Between Believers

1. *"Therefore"* links the way believers are to *"stand firm"* (4:1) with Christ's power. Describe this power (3:21).

    _____

    _____

    _____

2. How does Paul deal with the problem between Euodia and Syntyche (4:2-3)?

    _____

    _____

    _____

    _____

3. Paul refers to fellow believers whose names are written in *"the book of life."* What does this mean, and whose names are included according to Revelation 20:11-15 and 21:22-27?

    _____

    _____

    _____

❖ Philippians 4:4-7—Promise of Peace That Passes Understanding

4. Explain the relationship between Paul's instructions to show *"reasonableness ... to everyone"* and knowing that God is near (4:5).

   _____

   _____

5. a. What does Paul suggest as alternatives to worrying or being anxious?

   _____

   _____

   b. What does Jesus teach concerning anxiety? (See Matthew 6:25-33.)

   _____

   _____

   _____

   c. What exciting condition and promise does Jesus offer in Matthew 6:33?

   _____

   _____

6. What does Paul promise as the result of bringing our anxiety to God in prayer (Philippians 4:7)?

   _____

   _____

❖ Philippians 4:8-9—Pattern for Thinking and Acting

7. We experience God's promised peace through a transformed thought life. List eight qualities believers are to concentrate on.

   _____

   _____

8. Romans 12:1-2 gives a principle for transforming your thought life. What do you think it means?

9. In what practical ways could you establish positive thought patterns? (See also Ephesians 4:22-24.)

10. Read James 1:22-25. Why is it important to *"practice"* (Philippians 4:9) what you learn?

❖ Philippians 4:10-13—Paul's Secret of Contentment

11. a. Paul has experienced being *"brought low"* and having plenty (4:12). How has he *"learned in whatever situation … to be content"* (4:11)?

    b. Paul's use of the word *learn* implies a process and effort. Is that encouraging or discouraging to you? Why?

12. a. In 4:13, Paul says, *"I can do all things through Him who strengthens me."* In what areas of your life do you most need strength right now?

b.   How have you experienced God strengthening you in the past?

_____

_____

_____

❖ **Philippians 4:14-23—Paul's Gratitude Expressed**

13. a.   What have the Philippians shared with Paul? (See also 1:5, 7.)

_____

_____

b.   What is Paul's desire for them as they now share material gifts (4:17)?

_____

_____

14. Read 4:19. How have you seen God providing for your needs?

_____

_____

 Apply what you have learned. Make a small sign based on Philippians 4:8. It could say something like, Is it true?
> Is it honorable?
> Is it just?
> Is it pure? Etc.

You may want to look up the meanings of these words and rephrase the questions.

Tape this sign to your bathroom mirror, and use it to measure your thoughts as you get ready in the morning and prepare for bed at night.

Unity and Charity
Philippians 4

Paul challenged the Philippians to recognize that maturity and contentment do not come instantly. He was in process, and so were they. As their spiritual father, Paul urged them to develop their potential (Philippians 3:16). Although he was their teacher and mentor, he recognized them as his brothers and appealed to them to live in unity. There should be no sibling rivalry among God's children.

An Appeal for Unity

Conflict between Euodia and Syntyche is causing strife in the church, and Paul urges the women to reconcile quickly. He handles the situation diplomatically, recognizing the two as fellow workers with him. He asks the congregation to help them resolve their disagreement.

Conflict between believers leads to sin and weakens their witness. In all Paul's letters, he advises his readers to love and be patient with each other. He has already made it clear in this letter that he believes the well-being of the church should come before individual interests (Philippians 2:2-4).

Rejoicing and Prayer

Again, Paul urges the Philippians to *"Rejoice"* (4:4) and *"let your reasonableness be known to everyone"* (4:5). The word translated *"reasonableness"* means being *fair, reasonable,* and *forbearing.* It goes beyond justice to show mercy to the guilty—a prominent attribute of our just and merciful God. *"Be known"* refers to experiential or personal knowledge. The world appreciates Christianity only when it can see and experience the qualities of Christ in the lives of His followers. As Jesus taught His disciples, *"You are the salt of the earth. ... You are the light of the world"* (Matthew 5:13-14).

Think about being salt and light. Our job is to demonstrate our faith, not just talk about it. As salt once preserved meat before refrigeration, Christians act as a preservative for society. We shed light by letting other people see Christ in us. Can you think of someone you know who acts as salt and light where he or she lives? What is that person's impact?

Paul encourages his brothers by saying, *"The Lord is at hand"* (Philippians 4:5). *"At hand"* could refer to Christ's second coming, which has been the hope of the church for centuries (Titus 2:13). Or Paul may mean that God is close, not distant. In Philippians 4:6, he tells the Philippians not to *"be anxious about anything."* Instead, he urges them to *"let your requests be made known to God."* As we share our desires with God, the Giver of all good things, He will guard our thinking and give us peace beyond understanding.

Think about God's peace, a peace that can fill our lives. Like the joy of the Lord, it does not depend on circumstances. We can have God's peace even when surrounded by turmoil. This peace is a gift beyond our understanding. Without God, peace depends on the absence of trouble or on an unusually tranquil or strong personality. The peace God gives is dependent on God alone. When we reach out to claim it through our grateful prayers, God protects our hearts and minds against worry. And, although our prayers may not be answered exactly as we like, we will have peace.

Prescription for Spiritual Health

Although God gives peace, believers play a part in developing healthy thought patterns. In 4:8, Paul outlines eight qualities his readers should think about:

❖ *"whatever is true,"* the Lord is truth (John 14:6), and as His followers, we must follow the truth

❖ *"honorable,"* not crude, but awe-inspiring, reputable

❖ *"just,"* fair, right

- ❖ *"pure,"* sanctified, innocent
- ❖ *"lovely,"* friendly
- ❖ *"commendable,"* well spoken of
- ❖ *"excellence,"* above reproach, virtuous
- ❖ *"worthy of praise,"* commended by God

Because these qualities characterize Paul's life, he can say, *"What you have learned and received and heard and seen in me—practice these things"* (4:9).

Rejoicing at All Times

Having dared to tell the Philippians to do as he did, Paul gives them another example of right actions and attitudes to follow. He writes of his delight that they have again shown concern for him, and adds, *"I have learned in whatever situation I am to be content"* (4:11). There is no hint of pride here; he freely confesses he had to *learn* to be content, implying that it was not easy. He shares that *"I can do all things through Him who strengthens me"* (4:13). For countless Christians, the encouraging words in this chapter provide support during dark hours. Such phrases as *"Rejoice in the Lord always ... do not be anxious about anything ... the God of peace will be with you. ... I can do all things through Him"* are words to cling to—like a lifeboat in a stormy sea.

Next, Paul thanks believers for sharing in his troubles by sending him aid, commending them for their previous contributions to his support, and thus to the support of the gospel. He assures them God will supply all their needs out of His plentiful riches in Christ. Paul feels such excitement at God's goodness and graciousness that his writings are full of poetic words of praise to God. Philippians, which begins and ends as a personal letter to Paul's partners in the gospel, is no exception: *"To our God and Father be glory forever and ever. Amen"* (4:20).

Farewell Message

"Caesar's household" (4:22) refers not only to those who lived within the Imperial Palace, but to those involved in the administration of the Roman Empire, either in Rome or outside the capital. Because of Paul's upbeat attitude and faithful witness, many of *"Caesar's household"* had come to know the Lord. God was faithful and gracious to Paul as he worked to build God's kingdom, even while in chains. Because he had so fully experienced God's grace, Paul could ask that the grace of the Lord be with the Philippians also. And with that thought, he closes this letter.

Personalize this lesson.

Paul was under house arrest, chained to a Roman guard, awaiting a possible death sentence when he wrote, *"I rejoiced in the Lord greatly"* (4:10) and told others to *"rejoice in the Lord always"* (4:4). Paul lived life to the fullest and had lasting joy despite his circumstances as he sought deeper fellowship with his Lord. Paul's letter to the Philippians can teach us how to live a joyful, content life serving the Lord.

Lack of contentment often springs from pursuing goals other than the ones God has for us. There may be nothing wrong with these goals, such as career success, marriage, or results in ministry. But if we focus on these desires instead of the higher goal of knowing Christ, we may end up frustrated and unhappy.

If you are struggling with a lack of contentment, try to identify what goal(s) for your life are being frustrated. Surrender these goals to God, and ask Him to help you focus on a goal that you can achieve no matter what your circumstances: growing closer to Jesus and knowing Him better.

Small Group Leader's Guide

While *Engaging God's Word* is great for personal study, it is generally even more effective and enjoyable when studied with others. Studying with others provides different perspectives and insights, care, prayer support, and fellowship that studying on your own does not. Depending on your personal circumstances, consider studying with your family or spouse, with a friend, in a Sunday school, with a small group at church, work, or in your neighborhood, or in a mentoring relationship.

In a traditional Community Bible Study class, your study would involve a proven four-step method: personal study, a small group discussion facilitated by a trained leader, a lecture covering the passage of Scripture, and a written commentary about the same passage. *Engaging God's Word* provides two of these four steps with the study questions and commentary. When you study with a group, you add another of these— the group discussion. And if you enjoy teaching, you could even provide a modified form of the fourth, the lecture, which in a small group setting might be better termed a wrap-up talk.

Here are some suggestions to help leaders facilitate a successful group study.

1. Decide how long you would like each group meeting to last. For a very basic study, without teaching, time for fellowship, or group prayer, plan on one hour. If you want to allow for fellowship before the meeting starts, add at least 15 minutes. If you plan to give a short teaching, add 15 or 20 minutes. If you also want time for group prayer, add another 10 or 15 minutes. Depending on the components you include for your group, each session will generally last between one and two hours.

2. Set a regular time and place to meet. Meeting in a church classroom or a conference room at work is fine. Meeting in a home is also a good option, and sometimes more relaxed and comfortable.

3. Publicize the study and/or personally invite people to join you.

4.   Begin praying for those who have committed to come. Continue to pray for them individually throughout the course of the study.

5.   Make sure everyone has his or her own book at least a week before you meet for the first time.

6.   Encourage group members to read the first lesson and do the questions before they come to the group meeting.

7.   Prepare your own lesson.

8.   Prepare your wrap-up talk, if you plan to give one. Here is a simple process for developing a wrap-up talk:

   a.   Divide the passage you are studying into two or three divisions. Jot down the verses for each division and describe the content of each with one complete sentence that answers the question, "What is the passage about?"

   b.   Decide on the central idea of your wrap-up talk. The central idea is the life-changing principle found in the passage that you believe God wants to implant in the hearts and minds of your group. The central idea answers the question, "What does God want us to learn from this passage?"

   c.   Provide one illustration that would make your central idea clear and meaningful to your group. This could be an illustration from your own life, or a story you've read or heard somewhere else.

   d.   Suggest one application that would help your group put the central idea into practice.

   e.   Choose an aim for your wrap-up talk. The aim answers the question, "What does God want us to do about it?" It encourages specific change in your group's lives, if they choose to respond to the central idea of the passage. Often it takes the form of a question you will ask your group: "Will you, will I choose to … ?"

9. Show up early to the study so you can arrange the room, set up the refreshments (if you are serving any), and welcome people as they arrive.

10. Whether your meeting includes a fellowship time or not, begin the discussion time promptly each week. People appreciate it when you respect their time. Transition into the discussion with prayer, inviting God to guide the discussion time and minister personally to each person present.

11. Model enthusiasm to the group. Let them know how excited you are about what you are learning—and your eagerness to hear what God is teaching them.

12. As you lead through the questions, encourage everyone to participate, but don't force anyone. If one or two people tend to dominate the discussion, encourage quieter ones to participate by saying something like, "Let's hear from someone who hasn't shared yet." Resist the urge to teach during discussion time. This time is for your group to share what they have been discovering.

13. Try to allow time after the questions have been discussed to talk about the "Apply what you have learned," "Think about" and "Personalize this lesson" sections. Encourage your group members in their efforts to partner with God in allowing Him to transform their lives.

14. Transition into the wrap-up talk, if you are doing one (see number 8).

15. Close in prayer. If you have structured your group to allow time for prayer, invite group members to pray for themselves and one another, especially focusing on the areas of growth they would like to see in their lives as a result of their study. If you have not allowed time for group prayer, you as leader can close this time.

16. Before your group finishes their final lesson, start praying and planning for what your next *Engaging God's Word* study will be.

About Community Bible Study

For almost 40 years Community Bible Study has taught the Word of God through in-depth, community-based Bible studies. With nearly 700 classes in the United States as well as classes in more than 70 countries, Community Bible Study purposes to be an "every-person's Bible study, available to all."

Classes for men, women, youth, children, and even babies, are all designed to make members feel loved, cared for, and accepted—regardless of age, ethnicity, socio-economic status, education, or church membership. Because Bible study is most effective in one's heart language, Community Bible Study curriculum has been translated into more than 50 languages.

Community Bible Study makes every effort to stand in the center of the mainstream of historic Christianity, concentrating on the essentials of the Christian faith rather than denominational distinctives. Community Bible Study respects different theological views, preferring to focus on helping people to know God through His Word, grow deeper in their relationships with Jesus, and be transformed into His likeness.

Community Bible Study's focus ... is to glorify God by providing in-depth Bible studies and curriculum in a Christ-centered, grace-filled, and philosophically safe environment.

Community Bible Study's passion ... is the transformation of individuals, families, communities, and generations through the power of God's Word, making disciples of the Lord Jesus Christ.

Community Bible Study's relationship with local churches ... is one of support and respect. Community Bible Study classes are composed of people from many different churches; they are designed to complement and not compete with the ministry of the local church. Recognizing that the Lord has chosen the local church as His primary channel of ministry, Community Bible Study encourages class members to belong to and actively support their local churches and to be servants and leaders in their congregations.

Do you want to experience lasting transformation in your life? Are you ready to go deeper in God's Word? There is probably a Community Bible Study near you! Find out by visiting www.findmyclass.org or scan the QR code on this page.

For more information:

Call   800-826-4181

Email info@communitybiblestudy.org

Web   www.communitybiblestudy.org

Class   www.findmyclass.org

Where will your next Bible study adventure take you?

Engage Bible Studies help you discover the joy and the richness of God's Word and apply it your life.

Check out these titles for your next adventure:

Engaging God's Word: Genesis

Engaging God's Word: Daniel

Engaging God's Word: Luke

Engaging God's Word: Galatians

Engaging God's Word: Ephesians

Engaging God's Word: Colossians

Engaging God's Word: Hebrews

Engaging God's Word: 1 & 2 Peter

Engaging God's Word: James

Engaging God's Word: Revelation

Available at Amazon.com and in fine bookstores.

Visit engagebiblestudies.com